Great food FOR KIDS

Great Food for Kids is a cookbook with a difference: the recipes were chosen by children for children; children helped to test them and it was the majority view that decided what should be included.

The result is a well-balanced selection of recipes for all ages and all occasions. Brains with parsley sauce and tripe and onions got the thumbs down, but the panel approved plenty of salads, wholefood bakes, fruity desserts and vegetarian dishes alongside old favourites like hamburgers, pizza, pasta, chilli con carne, chicken drumsticks and sweet treats such as chocolate brownies and fudge.

Breakfasts and lunches came in for careful scrutiny, with the accent on speedily-prepared dishes for schooldays and some special treats for weekends. Suppers are more substantial, but also take into account the pit-stop factor; some dishes can be made in minutes while others can safely be put on hold for latecomers.

Teenagers had the strongest opinions. Their section ranges from spicy curries to crisp salads. It was they who were particularly concerned about nutrition. This was also the group with most vegetarians.

Finally, everyone had fun choosing the party food. Drinks, nibbles, savouries and sweet treats were all enthusiastically selected and sampled.

CONTENTS

BREAKFASTS AND LUNCHES

Every parent knows the value of giving children a good start each day, but in the early morning maelstrom it is all too easy to take the line of least resistance and offer sugary cereal. This chapter suggests vitamin and protein-packed alternatives - and takes a careful look at another neglected area, lunch.

Quick Muesli

This muesli will keep for several weeks in an airtight container.

375g (12oz) bran or oat flakes

375g (12oz) Allbran breakfast cereal

220g (7oz) rolled oats

60g (2oz) walnuts

90g (3oz) no-need-to-soak dried apricots, chopped

90g (3oz) sultanas

45g (1¹/₂oz) dried apple rings, chopped

1 Preheat oven to 180°C (350°F/Gas 4). Combine bran or oat flakes, Allbran and rolled oats in a large bowl.

2 Spread out the nuts on a baking sheet and toast in the oven for 5 minutes. When cool, chop and add to cereal.

3 Add dried fruit; mix well. Store in an airtight container. Serve with milk, yogurt or fruit juice.

Makes about 1.1kg (2¹/₂lb)

Variations
Use almonds instead of walnuts and vary the dried fruit by using figs, pears or pitted prunes. Wheat, barley, millet or rye flakes may be substituted for part of the cereal base.

Banana Porridge

300ml (10fl oz) semi-skimmed milk

300ml (10fl oz) water

110g (3¹/₂oz) rolled oats

pinch salt, optional

1-2 bananas, mashed

1 Combine milk and water in a heavy-based saucepan. Stir in oats and salt, if using.

2 Bring to the boil, stirring constantly, then simmer, stirring from time to time, for 6-8 minutes or until the porridge thickens.

3 Remove from the heat and stir in the mashed banana. Serve with hot milk or yogurt and honey.

Serves 3-4

Baked Eggs

60g (2oz) butter

60g (2oz) cooked ham, finely chopped

salt

freshly ground black pepper

4 eggs

4 tblspn single cream

chopped fresh parsley for garnish

1 Preheat oven to 190°C (375°F/Gas 5). Divide the butter between 4 ramekins placed in a roasting tin. Add boiling water to the tin so that it comes halfway up the sides of the ramekins, then transfer the tin to the oven until the butter has melted.

2 Divide the ham between the ramekins, add salt and pepper to taste and carefully break an egg into each. Spoon 1 tblspn cream over each egg.

3 Return the tin to the oven and bake for 6-10 minutes, until whites are firm but yolks remain soft. Garnish and serve at once.

Serves 4

Creamy Ham and Asparagus Soufflé Omelette

60g (2oz) cooked ham, finely chopped

30g (1oz) drained canned asparagus, chopped

2 tblspn grated Cheddar cheese

3 tblspn soured cream

1 tblspn snipped chives

3 eggs, separated

2 tblspn water

¹/₄ tspn freshly ground black pepper, optional

30g (1oz) butter

1 Preheat grill. Make filling by combining ham, asparagus, cheese, soured cream and chives in a bowl. Set aside. Mix egg yolks, water and pepper, if using, in a large jug. Stir thoroughly.

2 Beat egg whites until fluffy; fold into yolk mixture. Melt butter in a medium frying pan (with flameproof handle) until bubbling. Add egg mixture, tilting pan to cover completely. Cook for about 3 minutes over moderate heat until underside is golden.

3 Place pan under grill for about 1 minute until top of omelette is set. Spoon filling over one half of omelette, fold other half over and serve at once.

Serves 1-2

Saturday Sausage Sticks

8 chipolata sausages

8 cherry tomatoes, halved

8 button mushrooms

2 tblspn sweet chutney

1 Preheat grill. Cut sausages into 2cm (³/₄in) pieces.

2 Thread sausage lengths onto metal skewers alternately with tomato halves and mushrooms. Brush with chutney.

3 Grill sausage sticks for 10 minutes or until sausages are fully cooked, turning once.
Serves 4

Variations

Squares of red, green or yellow pepper, pineapple cubes and cubes of green or red-skinned apple make good additions to these tasty sticks.

Tomato Cheese Puffs

2 tomatoes, sliced into 8 slices

15g (¹/₂oz) butter

1 small onion, finely chopped

125g (4oz) Cheddar cheese, grated

4 eggs, beaten

100ml (3¹/₂fl oz) natural low fat yogurt

1 tspn flour

1 Preheat oven to 180°C (350°F/Gas 4). Place 1 tomato slice in the base of each of four 250ml (8fl oz) ovenproof dishes standing on a baking sheet.

2 Melt butter in a small frying pan and sauté onion until tender. Divide the onion between the dishes and sprinkle with half the cheese.

3 Beat the eggs, yogurt and flour together. Divide the mixture between the dishes and top each with a tomato slice. Sprinkle with remaining cheese. Bake for 30 minutes. Serve at once.
Serves 4

Scrambled Eggs with Corn

15g (¹/₂oz) butter

4 eggs, beaten

125g (4oz) canned cream-style sweetcorn

1 tbspn chopped fresh parsley

2 tblspn grated Red Leicester cheese

wholemeal toast to serve

1 Melt the butter in a heavy-based saucepan. Add the eggs, sweetcorn, parsley and cheese.

2 Cook over moderate heat, stirring frequently, until the eggs are soft, creamy and just beginning to set.

3 Serve at once, with hot buttered wholemeal toast.

Kitchen Tips

Try spreading the toast with a thin layer of yeast extract or a similar spread.

If the saucepan proves difficult to clean, fill it with cold water and set it aside for 30 minutes.

Fresh Fruit with Yogurt and Honey

2 bananas

1 tblspn orange or lemon juice

3 oranges, peeled and segmented

90g (3oz) raspberries

250ml (8fl oz) natural low fat yogurt

1 tblspn clear honey

1 Slice bananas into a medium bowl, sprinkle with orange or lemon juice and toss lightly.

2 Arrange the banana slices, orange segments and raspberries in serving dishes.

3 Divide the yogurt between the dishes and drizzle each portion with honey.
Serves 4

Fresh Fruit with Yogurt and Honey

French Toast Triangles

1 egg

60ml (2fl oz) milk

15g (¹/₂oz) butter

3 slices bread, halved diagonally

1 Combine the egg and milk in a shallow bowl. Mix well with a fork. Melt the butter in a frying pan over moderate heat.

2 Soak 2-3 bread triangles in the egg mixture for about 30 seconds on each side. Using a fish slice, transfer the bread to the frying pan.

3 Cook until the underside of each bread triangle is golden, then turn over and cook the other side. Drain on paper towels. Keep hot while cooking the rest of the triangles. Serve at once, with a savoury sauce or honey.

Makes 6 triangles

Healthy Banana and Malt Milkshake

500ml (16fl oz) milk

2 bananas, sliced

1 tblspn clear honey

1 tblspn natural bran

2 tspn wheatgerm

1 tblspn malt drink powder

¹/₂ tspn vanilla essence, optional

Combine all the ingredients in a blender or food processor and blend until smooth.

Serves 2

Kitchen Tip

Add extra protein to this drink, and transform it into a meal-in-a-glass for a busy teenager, by adding 1 or 2 eggs. The eggs must be very fresh and from a reputable source. Do not give raw egg in any form to young children.

Dried Fruit Salad

Dried Fruit Salad

30g (1oz) pitted dried prunes

60g (2oz) dried apricots, halved

3 bananas

45g (1¹/₂oz) sultanas

¹/₂ tspn grated lemon rind

15g (¹/₂oz) butter, melted

2 tblspn clear honey mixed with 2 tblspn boiling water

250ml (8fl oz) freshly squeezed orange juice

1 Put the prunes and apricots in an ovenproof dish. Add water to cover. Soak overnight; drain.

2 Preheat oven to 180°C (350°F/Gas 4). Slice the bananas and add them to the dish with the sultanas, lemon rind, butter and honey mixture. Mix well.

3 Cover the dish with foil and bake for 35 minutes. Add the orange juice and bake for 5 minutes more. Serve hot or cold, with Greek yogurt if liked.

Serves 4

Cheesy Salmon Patties

315g (10oz) drained canned butterbeans

1 x 200g (6½oz) can red salmon, drained, bones and skin removed

125g (4oz) mashed potato

90g (3oz) Cheddar cheese, grated

30g (1oz) grated Parmesan cheese

1 small onion, finely chopped

1 tblspn finely snipped chives

60g (2oz) flour

2 tblspn lemon juice

1 egg, lightly beaten

60g (2oz) dried breadcrumbs

oil for deep frying

1 Mash butterbeans and salmon to a paste. Add potato, cheeses, onion, chives, flour and lemon juice. Mix well, then add enough egg to bind.

2 Divide mixture evenly into 6-8 portions and form each into a patty. Toss each patty in breadcrumbs until evenly covered.

3 Heat the oil in a large frying pan. Add the patties, pressing them down with a fish slice to flatten. Cook for 2 minutes on each side until golden.
Makes 6-8

Bacon and Bean Bake

250g (8oz) rindless streaky bacon rashers

1 onion, chopped

125ml (4fl oz) tomato ketchup

45g (1½oz) soft brown sugar

1 tblspn red wine vinegar

1 tblspn Dijon mustard

470g (15oz) drained canned red kidney beans

470g (15oz) drained canned butterbeans

1 Preheat oven to 180°C (350°F/Gas 4). Heat bacon in a frying pan until the fat runs, then increase the heat and fry for about 5 minutes or until crisp. Using a slotted spoon, transfer to paper towels to drain.

Cheesy Salmon Patties

2 Add the onion to the fat remaining in the pan. Fry for about 5 minutes, stirring occasionally, until golden. Tip contents of pan into a bowl; add ketchup, sugar, vinegar and mustard.

3 Crumble the bacon into the bowl and stir in all the beans. Transfer mixture to an ovenproof serving dish.

4 Bake for about 30 minutes or until beans are heated through and bubbly. Serve hot.
Serves 4-6

Macaroni and Cauliflower Cheese

250g (8oz) elbow macaroni

1 small cauliflower, divided into florets

50g (2oz) butter

50g (2oz) flour

600ml (1pt) milk

125g (4oz) grated Red Leicester cheese

1 tblspn wheatgerm

1 Preheat oven to 180°C (350°F/Gas 4). Cook the macaroni in a large saucepan of boiling salted water until tender or *al dente*. Drain well.

2 Boil, steam or microwave cauliflower florets until just tender; drain, then place in a shallow ovenproof dish. Add the macaroni and mix lightly.

3 Melt the butter in a small saucepan, stir in the flour and cook for 1 minute. Gradually add the milk, stirring until sauce boils and thickens. Off heat, stir in half the cheese.

4 Pour the sauce over the macaroni and cauliflower mixture; stir lightly. Sprinkle with remaining cheese and wheatgerm. Bake for 15 minutes. Serve at once.
Serves 4

Cheesy Oatburgers

125g (4oz) Cheddar cheese, grated
1/4 green pepper, finely chopped
1 tomato, finely chopped
1 small onion, finely chopped
110g (3½oz) rolled oats
2 eggs, lightly beaten
45g (1½oz) flour
oil for shallow frying

1 Combine cheese, green pepper, tomato, onion, oats, eggs and flour in a medium bowl. Mix well. Divide mixture into 6 portions and shape into patties.

2 Heat the oil in a large frying pan. Add the patties, pressing them down with a fish slice to flatten. Cook for 3 minutes on each side until golden.

3 Serve each oatburger on a wholemeal roll with salad.
Makes 6

Filled Jacket Potatoes with Mushrooms and Cheese

4 large baking potatoes, scrubbed and dried
1 tblspn olive oil
1 small onion, finely chopped
250g (8oz) mushrooms, sliced
1 clove garlic, crushed, optional
1 tblspn flaked almonds, toasted
125g (4oz) cottage cheese
125ml (4fl oz) natural low fat yogurt
1 tblspn chopped fresh parsley

1 Preheat oven to 200°C (400°F/Gas 6). Prick potatoes all over with a skewer. Place the potatoes directly on the oven shelf and bake for 1-1¼ hours until tender.

2 Cut the potatoes in half. Scoop the flesh into a bowl, leaving a 1cm (½in) thick potato shell. Using a little of the oil, brush potato shells inside and out. Arrange the shells on a baking sheet and return them to the oven for 10 minutes.

3 Heat the remaining oil in a saucepan, add the onion and cook for 5 minutes, stirring occasionally. Add mushrooms, with garlic if using, and cook for 5 minutes more.

4 Mash the potatoes. Add the onion mixture with the almonds, cottage cheese, yogurt and parsley.

5 Spoon the filling into the potato shells, piling it up in the centre. Return to the oven for 15-20 minutes to heat through. Serve at once.
Serves 4

Best Ever Hamburgers

The finest hamburgers are made from good quality minced steak with no addition other than a little grated onion, if liked. This, however, makes them a luxury item. The mixture may be stretched by the addition of a small quantity of breadcrumbs, finely grated carrot or wheatgerm. For extra flavour, add 1 tspn Worcestershire or soy sauce, or mushroom ketchup.

500g (1lb) minced steak
salt
freshly ground black pepper
1 tblspn finely chopped onion, optional

1 Preheat the grill. Mix all the ingredients together in a medium bowl. Divide mixture into 4-6 portions and shape into patties.

2 Grill the burgers for about 4 minutes on each side or until done to your taste.

3 Serve in burger baps, with salad and relish or ketchup.
Serves 4-6

Cheesy Oatburgers

Vanilla Ice Cream

Vanilla Ice Cream

75g (2¹/₂oz) caster sugar

75ml (2¹/₂fl oz) water

1 tspn powdered gelatine

60g (2oz) skim milk powder

500ml (16fl oz) semi-skimmed milk

1 tspn white vinegar

2 tspn vanilla essence

1 Combine sugar and water in a small saucepan. Add gelatine and stir constantly over gentle heat until both sugar and gelatine have dissolved.

2 Transfer mixture to a large bowl, whisk in milk powder, then gradually beat in milk, using a hand-held electric mixer.

3 Spoon into 2 shallow freezerproof containers and freeze for about 1 hour or until crystals form around the edges.

4 Tip both mixtures into a large bowl, add the vinegar and vanilla essence and beat until thick and creamy. Return to containers and freeze for 3 hours or overnight.

5 To serve, scoop the ice cream into small cone cups. Top with candy-coated chocolate beans and hundreds and thousands, if liked.
Makes about 1.5 litres (2¹/₂pt)

Kitchen Tip
Remember to turn the freezer or refrigerator freezing compartment to the coldest setting about 1 hour before adding the ice cream. When the ice cream is firm, return the setting to its normal position.

The ice cream will be easier to scoop and will have a fuller flavour if it is transferred from the freezer to the refrigerator about 15 minutes before serving.

Apple and Blackberry Crumble

500g (1lb) cooking apples, peeled and sliced

90g (3oz) sugar

45ml (1¹/₂fl oz) water

250g (8oz) blackberries

125g (4oz) flour

60g (2oz) caster sugar

60g (2oz) butter, cubed

1 Preheat oven to 180°C (350°F/Gas 4). Combine apples, sugar and water in a small saucepan. Cook, covered, until apples are tender. Spoon into a baking dish, add blackberries and mix lightly.

2 Mix flour and sugar in a bowl. Add butter and rub it in until mixture resembles fine bread-crumbs. Sprinkle over fruit and bake for 20 minutes.
Serves 4

Keep suppers simple with satisfying dishes which will appeal to all members of the family. Recipes in this chapter range from quick grills like Sausage Rollers and Herbed Lamb Patties to slow-cooked casseroles and bakes for more leisurely evenings. Vegetarians are well catered for, and simple puddings and pancakes add a final flourish.

Spaghetti with Meat Sauce

For older children, add 1 tspn dried basil or oregano to the sauce or use canned tomatoes with herbs.

250g (8oz) spaghetti
salt
grated Parmesan cheese for garnish

Sauce

1 tblspn oil
1 onion, finely chopped
1 small carrot, grated
1 clove garlic, crushed, optional
500g (1lb) lean minced beef
2 x 397g (14oz) cans chopped tomatoes
1 x 64g (2oz) can tomato purée
250ml (8fl oz) beef stock
freshly ground black pepper

1 First make the sauce. Heat the oil in a heavy-based saucepan, add the onion and carrot and fry over gentle heat for 4-5 minutes, stirring occasionally. Add the garlic, if using, and cook for 2 minutes more. Transfer the vegetable mixture to a bowl; set aside.

2 Add the mince to the pan. Fry, stirring constantly, until lightly browned and cooked through. Drain off excess fat.

3 Return the vegetable mixture to the pan and stir in the tomatoes and tomato purée. Add the stock. Bring to the boil, then lower the heat and simmer for 30 minutes. Add salt and pepper to taste. If a smoother sauce is preferred, process briefly in a blender or food processor.

4 Cook the spaghetti in boiling salted water until tender or *al dente*. Drain.

5 Serve the spaghetti topped with the meat sauce and a sprinkling of Parmesan cheese.
Serves 4-6

Pork Fillet and Apple Casserole

45g (1¹/₂oz) butter
1 onion, finely chopped
500g (1lb) pork fillet, trimmed, cut into 2cm (³/₄in) cubes
3 large cooking apples, peeled and sliced
1 carrot, cut into thin strips
750ml (1¹/₄pt) chicken stock
1 bay leaf
1 tspn dried savory, optional
250g (8oz) canned chopped tomatoes
2 eating apples, cubed
mint to garnish

1 Melt 30g (1oz) of the butter in a large frying pan. Add the onion and pork and cook, stirring, for 5 minutes. Drain excess fat and add cooking apples, carrot, stock, bay leaf and savory, if using. Bring to the boil, then simmer for 1 hour or until pork is tender and cooked through. Using a slotted spoon, transfer pork cubes to a bowl; keep hot.

2 Transfer mixture remaining in pan to a food processor. Discard bay leaf. Purée mixture, then press through a sieve into a clean pan. Add reserved pork and tomatoes and heat through.

3 Melt remaining butter in a frying pan and sauté apple cubes gently until cooked. Transfer pork mixture to a serving dish, stir in apple cubes, garnish with mint and serve at once.
Serves 4

Pork Fillet and Apple Casserole

Herbed Lamb Patties

15g (½oz) butter

2 cloves garlic, crushed

4 spring onions, finely chopped

750g (1½lb) minced lamb

1 tspn chopped fresh thyme

1 tspn chopped fresh rosemary

2 tspn chopped fresh parsley

1 tblspn lemon juice

1 tblspn tomato purée

3 tblspn fresh breadcrumbs

1 Preheat grill. Melt the butter in a small frying pan over moderate heat. Add the garlic and spring onions and cook for 1 minute.

2 Tip the mixture into a bowl and add the remaining ingredients. Mix well.

3 Shape the mixture into 12 patties. Grill for 3-4 minutes on each side until cooked through. Serve with a garnish of fresh herbs, if liked.
Serves 4

Creamy Whipped Potato and Carrot

3 large potatoes, quartered

1 large carrot, sliced

salt

30g (1oz) butter

4 tblspn single cream or creamy milk

1 Cook the potatoes and carrot in separate saucepans of boiling salted water until very tender. Drain.

2 Mix the vegetables together and mash lightly, then add the butter and cream. Whip, using a hand-held electric mixer, until fluffy. Serve at once.
Serves 4

Vegetable Sauté with Feta

60ml (2fl oz) oil

3 carrots, cut into thin strips

1 onion, chopped

1 aubergine, cut into 2cm (3/4in) cubes

1 red pepper, cut into strips

1 tlbspn red wine vinegar

155g (5oz) feta, crumbled

herb sprig for garnish

1 Heat the oil in a large frying pan, add the carrots and onion and cook for 2 minutes, stirring constantly.

2 Add the aubergine and red pepper and sauté over moderately high heat for 3 minutes. Stir in the vinegar and cook for 1 minute more.

3 Spoon mixture into a serving dish, top with feta, garnish and serve.
Serves 4

Baked Beans with Sausages

2 x 447g (14 3/4oz) cans baked beans in tomato sauce

1 stick celery, chopped

125g (4oz) button mushrooms, sliced

1 green pepper, chopped

1 x 339g (12oz) can pineapple chunks, drained

1 tspn Worcestershire sauce

200g (7oz) chipolata sausages, grilled

1 Preheat oven to 180°C (350°F/ Gas 4). Mix beans, celery, mushrooms, pepper and pineapple chunks in an ovenproof dish. Stir in Worcestershire sauce.

2 Chop sausages into 1cm (1/2in) lengths. Add to bean mixture.

3 Bake, uncovered, for 30 minutes or until sausages are cooked through. Serve.
Serves 6

Vegetable Sauté with Feta

Baked Fish and Tomato Gratin

15g (1/2oz) butter, melted

750g (1 1/2lb) cod fillets, skinned

250g (8oz) mature Cheddar cheese, grated

4 tomatoes, sliced

1 tblspn finely chopped fresh basil

salt

freshly ground black pepper

1 Preheat oven to 180°C (350°F/Gas 4). Grease an ovenproof dish with butter. Arrange half the fish in dish, sprinkle with one-third of the cheese and top with half the tomatoes. Dust with basil, salt and pepper.

2 Top with the rest of the fish, half remaining cheese and the rest of the tomatoes. Season and top with remaining cheese. Bake for 30 minutes. Serve at once.
Serves 6

Sausage Rollers

3 large pitta breads

6 thick pork sausages

6 no-need-to-soak dried apricots, halved

3 rindless streaky bacon rashers

1 large carrot, grated

1/2 small lettuce, shredded

60g (2oz) beansprouts

125g (4oz) Cheddar cheese, grated

1 Preheat grill. Cut each pitta bread in half and open out the pockets.

2 Cut a slit in the side of each sausage, place 2 apricot halves in each, wrap in half a bacon rasher and secure with a wooden cocktail stick. Grill until cooked through, then remove toothpicks.

3 Tuck a sausage into each pitta pocket and add carrot, lettuce, beansprouts and cheese. Serve.
Serves 6

Lentil and Vegetable Cottage Pie

250g (8oz) brown lentils

2 bay leaves

1 tblspn oil

1 onion, chopped

4 carrots, chopped

2 celery sticks, chopped

1 tspn dried mixed herbs

1 tblspn chopped fresh parsley

1 x 397g (14oz) can chopped tomatoes

2 tblspn tomato purée

4 large potatoes, quartered

salt

30g (1oz) butter

3-4 tblspn milk

1 Put the lentils in a saucepan with the bay leaves. Add water to cover, bring to the boil, then simmer for 30 minutes until almost tender. Remove bay leaves and set lentils aside.

2 Preheat oven to 180°C (350°F/Gas 4). Heat the oil in a large frying pan. Add the onion, carrots and celery and cook for 4-5 minutes over moderate heat.

3 Stir in the lentils, herbs, parsley, chopped tomatoes and tomato purée. Cover and simmer for 15 minutes, adding a little water if the mixture is too thick.

4 Meanwhile cook the potatoes in a saucepan of boiling salted water until tender. Drain and mash with the butter and milk.

5 Spoon the lentil mixture into a large ovenproof dish. Top with the mashed potato, using a fork to mark it with a wavy design. Bake for 30 minutes.
Serves 6

Kitchen Tip
Brown lentils are used for this bake because they retain their shape. Red lentils can be used, but require only 15 minutes cooking time in Step 1.

Oven Fried Chicken

If you prefer to avoid giving chicken bones to very young children, use chicken breasts instead.

6 chicken drumsticks

150ml (5fl oz) natural low fat yogurt

1 tspn lemon juice

2 tblspn apricot or peach chutney

125g (4oz) packaged dried breadcrumbs

parsley sprigs for garnish

1 Preheat oven to 180°C (350°F/Gas 4). Purée the yogurt, lemon juice and chutney in a blender or food processor; transfer to a shallow bowl. Spread out the breadcrumbs in a similar bowl.

2 Coat each drumstick in yogurt mixture, then roll in bread-crumbs. Arrange on a baking sheet and bake for 45 minutes or until cooked through. Garnish and serve.
Makes 6

Oven Fried Chicken

Pork, Sausage and Prosciutto Kebabs

Fish Pie

315g (10oz) cooked white fish, skin and bones removed

250g (8oz) mashed potato

185g (6oz) cooked carrots, mashed

1 tblspn chopped fresh parsley

4 tblspn fresh white breadcrumbs

2 tblspn melted butter

parsley sprig for garnish

1 Preheat oven to 180°C (350°F/Gas 4). Flake the fish, checking to ensure that no bones remain.

2 Combine mashed potato and carrots. Spread half the mixture over the base of a greased ovenproof dish.

3 Arrange the fish on top of the potato mixture, sprinkle with parsley and cover with the remaining potato mixture.

4 Sprinkle with breadcrumbs, drizzle with melted butter and bake for 15-20 minutes until the filling is hot and the topping lightly browned. Serve at once, garnished with parsley.
Serves 4

Pork, Sausage and Prosciutto Kebabs

4 spicy Italian sausages or frankfurters

250g (8oz) pork fillet, trimmed

1 red pepper, cut into 2cm (³/4in) squares

1 green pepper, cut into 2cm (³/4in) squares

5-6 drained canned baby corn cobs, halved

1/4 loaf day-old bread, crusts removed, cut into 2cm (³/4in) cubes

90g (3oz) thinly sliced prosciutto, cut into strips 2cm (³/4in) wide

1 Soak 8 wooden skewers in warm water for 1 hour.

2 Bring a large saucepan of water to the boil, add Italian sausages and cook for 8 minutes. If using frankfurters, omit this step.

3 Preheat grill. Drain sausages and cut into 2cm (³/4in) lengths. Cut pork fillet into 2cm (³/4in) cubes.

4 Thread red and green pepper squares, pork cubes, pieces of corn and sausages alternately onto the skewers, ending each skewer with a bread cube.

5 Grill kebabs, turning occasionally, until pork is cooked through.

6 Remove from the heat and wrap a piece of prosciutto around the pork cubes. Return the kebabs to the heat and grill for 1 minute more on each side. Serve at once.
Serves 4-8

Baked Apples with Walnut Crust

60g (2oz) walnut halves

60g (2oz) sugar

45g (1½oz) soft brown sugar

2 tspn ground cinnamon

4 green apples

60g (2oz) butter, melted

strawberry halves to decorate (optional)

cream or fromage frais for serving

1 Preheat oven to 180°C (350°F/Gas 4). Combine the walnuts, sugar, brown sugar and cinnamon in a blender or food processor; process until nuts are finely chopped.

2 Core the apples and peel two thirds of the skin from the top. Brush the exposed apple flesh with butter, then press the walnut sugar mixture onto it.

3 Arrange the apples in a baking dish and cook for 45 minutes until tender. Decorate if liked and serve with cream or fromage frais.
Serves 4

Pineapple Upside-down Cake

45g (1½oz) butter

90g (3oz) soft brown sugar

1 x 439g (14oz) can pineapple rings, drained

about 6 glacé cherries

Cake

250g (8oz) butter, softened

4 eggs

185g (6oz) soft brown sugar

185g (6oz) self-raising flour

2 tspn baking powder

60g (2oz) ground almonds

freshly squeezed juice of 1 orange

1 Melt the butter with the brown sugar in a small saucepan over gentle heat; mix well. Brush over the bottom of a well greased 25cm (10in) springform cake tin. Arrange

the pineapple rings in the tin, putting a cherry in the centre of each, and filling awkward places with halved or quartered rings. Set aside.

2 Preheat oven to 180°C (350°F/Gas 4). Make the cake by combining all the ingredients in a bowl and beating for 2 minutes with a hand-held electric mixer. Spread on top of the pineapple.

3 Bake for about 50 minutes or until the sides of the cake shrink away from the tin and an inserted skewer comes out clean. Cool in the tin for 10 minutes, then turn out onto a wire rack and cool completely.
Serves 8

Cherry Cobbler

2 x 425g (13½oz) cans stoned black cherries, drained

60g (2oz) soft brown sugar

30g (1oz) cornflour

Topping

175g (6oz) self-raising flour

1 tspn baking powder

40g (1½oz) butter

2 tbspn sugar

5-6 tblspn milk

1 Preheat oven to 220°C (425°F/Gas 7). Mix the cherries, sugar and cornflour in a 20cm (8in) square baking dish.

2 Make the topping. Combine the flour and baking powder in a mixing bowl. Rub in the butter until the mixture resembles fine breadcrumbs, then stir in the sugar and add just enough milk to make a soft dough.

3 Pat out the dough lightly on a floured surface and cut out 5cm (2in) round scones. Arrange the scones on top of the cherry mixture, brush with the remaining milk and bake for 12-15 minutes or until the scones are well risen and golden.
Serves 6

Baked Apples with Walnut Crust

Strawberry Jam Pancake Stack, Pancakes with Chocolate Filling

Pancakes with Chocolate Filling

155g (5oz) self-raising flour

1¹/₂ tblspn caster sugar

1 egg, lightly beaten

350ml (12fl oz) milk

Filling

125g (4oz) digestive biscuits

60g (2oz) butter

60g (2oz) soft brown sugar

3 tblspn drinking chocolate powder

90g (3oz) cream cheese

1 Sift flour into a medium bowl. Add the sugar. In a jug, beat egg with milk. Make a well in centre of the flour, add liquid mixture and gradually incorporate flour. If mixture is lumpy, process it briefly in a food processor or blender, or press through a strainer.

2 Pour 3 tablespoons of batter into a heated, well-greased pancake pan. Cook over moderate heat until golden underneath, then flip pancake over and cook other side until golden. Repeat with remaining batter. Set pancakes aside to cool.

3 Make filling: Crush biscuits coarsely in a food processor. Melt butter with sugar in a saucepan, then remove from heat and stir in drinking chocolate powder. Beat in the cream cheese, then stir in the crushed biscuits.

4 Spread each pancake with filling, roll up and serve at once, with strawberries if liked.
Serves 4-6

Pancake Fillings
Children love pancakes Here are some more suggestions for fillings:
● Poached apple slices with sultanas
● Sliced strawberries with *fromage frais* or whipped cream
● Bananas, mashed with a little brown sugar
● Lemon curd with sliced canned pears
● Drained mandarin oranges with Greek yogurt

Strawberry Jam Pancake Stack

155g (5oz) self-raising flour

3 eggs

2 tblspn caster sugar

250ml (8fl oz) buttermilk

30g (1oz) butter, melted

strawberry jam for spreading

icing sugar for dusting

cream or custard to serve

Decoration (optional)

60g (2oz) marzipan

food colouring

1 Sift the flour into a medium bowl. In a large jug, beat the eggs with the sugar until thick and pale, then stir in buttermilk and melted butter. Make a well in the centre of the flour, add the liquid mixture and gradually incorporate the flour. If the batter is lumpy, process it briefly in a food processor or blender, or press through a strainer.

2 Pour 3 tablespoons of the batter into a heated, well-greased pancake pan. Cook over moderate heat until golden underneath, then flip pancake over and cook other side until golden. Repeat with remaining mixture.

3 Stack the pancakes, spreading each layer with strawberry jam. Dust the top pancake with icing sugar.

4 Colour the marzipan and mould it into a flower shape for the decoration, if liked. Serve with cream or custard.
Serves 6

Peach Crêpes with Raspberry Sauce

Peach Crêpes with Raspberry Sauce

90g (3oz) flour

3 eggs

30g (1oz) butter, melted

250ml (8fl oz) milk

Filling

30g (1oz) butter

2 large peaches, skinned and thinly sliced

2 tblspn caster sugar

Sauce

250g (8oz) raspberries

1 tblspn lemon juice

4 tblspn raspberry jam

1 Sift the flour into a medium bowl. In a jug, beat the eggs with the melted butter and milk. Make a well in the centre of the flour, add the liquid mixture and gradually incorporate the flour. If the mixture is lumpy, process it briefly in a food processor or blender, or press through a strainer.

2 Pour 2 tablespoons of the batter into a heated, well-greased crêpe pan. Cook over moderate heat until golden underneath, then flip crêpe over and cook other side until golden. Repeat with remaining batter.

3 Make the filling: Melt the butter in a frying pan, add the peach slices and sauté lightly for 1-2 minutes. Fill the crêpes with peach slices, sprinkle lightly with caster sugar and roll up. Arrange the filled crêpes in a serving dish and keep hot.

4 Combine the raspberries, lemon juice and jam in a small saucepan. Heat gently for 5 minutes, then press the mixture through a sieve into a jug. Pour over the crêpes and serve at once.
Serves 6

Kitchen Tip
The easiest way to skin the peaches is to put them in a heatproof bowl, pour over boiling water to cover and set them aside for 2 minutes. Make a small cross in the skin on the top of each peach and slip the skins off.

PACKED WITH GOODNESS

Providing a packed lunch that is nutritious, satisfying and enjoyable enough to avoid being swapped for a chocolate bar and a bag of crisps is one of the challenges of the age. This chapter promises plenty of inspiration.

Pizza Squares

155g (5oz) wholemeal flour

155g (5oz) flour

1/2 tspn salt

1 x 7g (1/4oz) sachet easy blend dried yeast

2 tblspn oil

185ml (6fl oz) warm water

Topping

1 onion, chopped

1 tlbspn oil

1 x 397g (14oz) can chopped tomatoes, plain or with herbs

1 tblspn chopped fresh or l tspn dried basil, optional

3 tblspn tomato purée

125g (4oz) mushrooms, sliced

2 spring onions, sliced

125g (4oz) cooked ham, chopped, or 125g (4oz) grilled bacon, crumbled

8-12 pitted black olives, optional

125g (4oz) thinly sliced mozzarella or grated Cheddar cheese

1 Combine flours, salt and yeast in a large bowl. Stir in oil and warm water. Mix to a dough, then turn onto a lightly floured surface and knead for about 5 minutes until smooth and elastic.

2 Place the dough in an oiled bowl, cover with clingfilm and a tea towel. Stand in a warm place until doubled in bulk.

3 Knead the dough for 2 minutes, roll it out and use to line a lightly oiled 35 x 28cm (14 x 11in) Swiss roll tin.

4 Preheat oven to 190°C (375°F/Gas 5). Make the topping. Fry the onion in the oil for 5 minutes, add the tomatoes with the basil, if using, and simmer for 10 minutes; cool.

5 Spread the dough with the tomato purée, then cover with the onion and tomato mixture. Sprinkle evenly with mushrooms, spring onions, ham or bacon and olives, if using. Finally top with the cheese.

6 Bake for 20 minutes or until the pizza is well risen and the cheese topping is golden. Cool slightly, cut into 12 squares, then cool completely. Wrap squares in greaseproof paper or pack in a small polythene box for school.
Makes 12

Variations

Use the basic recipe above, adding the tomato purée and sauce, but vary the toppings. Try bacon and sweetcorn, ham and pineapple, drained tuna and mushrooms, peperoni and sliced red or green peppers.

For quick mini pizzas, use muffins or rounds of French bread as bases. Top as above.

Pizza Squares

SANDWICH FILLINGS

Sandwiches remain the top favourite for school packed lunches. Experiment with different breads, rolls or baps, try some of the fillings below or pack a filled pitta pocket.

● Cottage cheese and celery
● Thinly spread yeast extract with sliced cucumber
● Peanut butter and chopped dates or sultanas
● Tuna mixed with grated apple, a pinch of curry powder and a little mayonnaise
● Smoked turkey with chutney
● Sliced frankfurters with tomato

Vegetable Frittata Wedges

2 tblspn oil
1 onion, very thinly sliced
1 potato, very thinly sliced
salt
1 x 340g (11oz) can asparagus spears, drained
1 red pepper, cut into strips
1 courgette, sliced
6 eggs, beaten
freshly ground black pepper
2 tblspn grated Parmesan cheese

1 Preheat oven to 180°C (350°F/Gas 4). Pour the oil into a 23cm (9in) pie tin. Heat in the oven for 5 minutes, then spread the onion slices over the base of the tin. Top with the potato, sprinkle with salt, cover with foil and bake for 30 minutes or until vegetables are tender.

2 Arrange the asparagus, red pepper strips and courgette slices over the potato layer. Pour over the eggs, season with salt and pepper and sprinkle with cheese. Bake, uncovered, for 20 minutes or until set. Cool for 10 minutes before cutting into wedges.
Makes 8

Healthy Lunch Box Salad

Unless the salad is to be eaten within a very short time, pack the chilled vegetables and asparagus dressing separately.

1 Iceberg lettuce, torn into pieces

2 tomatoes, chopped

4 sticks celery, sliced

1/2 cucumber, chopped

125g (4oz) Cheddar cheese, grated

1 carrot, grated

2 tblspn snipped chives

2 tblspn lemon juice

2 hard-boiled eggs, quartered, for garnish

Asparagus Dressing

4 tblspn natural low fat yogurt

2 tblspn chopped fresh parsley

salt

freshly ground black pepper

375g (12oz) drained canned salad-cut asparagus

1 Combine lettuce, tomatoes, celery, cucumber, cheese, carrot and chives. Sprinkle with half the lemon juice, toss, cover and chill.

2 Make the dressing by mixing the yogurt and parsley in a bowl. Add the remaining lemon juice with salt and pepper to taste. Mix well, then stir in the asparagus.

3 Spoon the dressing over the chilled vegetables, garnish with the eggs and pack as suggested above.
Serves 4

Fruit and Cheese Salad

1 banana, sliced

1 tblspn lemon juice

2 tblspn flaked almonds toasted

1 small red apple (unskinned), chopped

1 small orange, peeled and cubed

1 small pear (unpeeled), chopped

60g (2oz) Edam or Gouda cheese, chopped

60ml (2fl oz) natural low fat yogurt

Toss banana slices in lemon juice. Combine all ingredients in a bowl. Spoon into lunch boxes. Refrigerate until required for school.
Serves 2-4

Mini Quiches

Pastry

250g (8oz) flour

pinch salt

185g (6oz) cold butter, cubed

75-90ml (2^1/$_2$-3fl oz) iced water

Filling

2 eggs, beaten

250ml (8fl oz) single cream or milk

salt

freshly ground black pepper

1 Make the pastry. Combine the flour and salt in a bowl and rub in the butter until the mixture resembles fine breadcrumbs. Add enough of the iced water to make a dough. Shape the dough to a flattish round, wrap and refrigerate for I hour.

2 On a lightly floured surface, roll out the dough to a thickness of about 2.5mm (1/8in). Cut into rounds and line about 24 small tartlet tins. Prick the base of each pastry case.

3 Preheat oven to 190°C (375°F/Gas 4). Mix the eggs and cream or milk in a jug, add salt and pepper to taste, and carefully pour the mixture into the tartlets, almost filling them.

4 Bake for 20-25 minutes, until the filling is set. When cold, wrap and pack carefully, using crumpled greaseproof paper if necessary to cushion the quiches while being transported.
Makes 24

Variations
Put a teasponful of salad-cut asparagus, sun-dried tomatoes, lightly fried mushrooms (alone or with bacon or ham), drained canned sweetcorn, ratatouille, chopped smoked salmon or lightly fried leeks to each mini quiche before baking, if liked.

Fruit, Nut and Cheese Salad

Celery Boats

Baked Bean Pasties

1 x 215g (7¹/₂oz) packet frozen shortcrust pastry, thawed

15g (¹/₂oz) butter

1 onion, sliced

2 rashers rindless streaky bacon, chopped

1 large carrot, finely chopped

1 x 220g (7³/₄oz) can baked beans in tomato sauce

125g (4oz) Cheddar cheese, grated

1 egg, beaten

1 Preheat oven to 190°C (375°F/Gas 5). Roll out the pastry and use an upside-down saucer to cut out 6 rounds.

2 Melt butter in a frying pan and fry onion, bacon and carrot until soft. Stir in baked beans. Cool.

3 Pile mixture into centre of pastry rounds. Top with cheese. Brush pastry edges with egg, then bring up sides to form a pasty. Flute edges to seal in the filling.

4 Place the pasties on a baking sheet, brush with beaten egg and bake for 25 minutes or until golden brown. Cool, then wrap and refrigerate until required for school.
Makes 6

Celery Boats

125g (4oz) cream cheese

75g (2¹/₂oz) peanut butter

4 sticks celery

sultanas

Beat the cream cheese and peanut butter together and fill celery 'boats'. Dot with sultanas. Cut each celery stick into 5cm (2in) lengths. Pack in polythene tubs. Refrigerate until required.
Serves 4

Filled Baguettes

2 baguettes, sliced lengthwise

185ml (6fl oz) French dressing

4 large tomatoes, thinly sliced

1 Spanish onion, thinly sliced

2 green peppers, thinly sliced

60g (2oz) thinly sliced salami

4 hard-boiled eggs, sliced

1 Brush cut sides of baguettes generously with French dressing. Set 'lids' aside and top base with tomato, onion and green pepper. Top with slices of salami and egg.

2 Press lids onto bases; wrap filled baguettes tightly in foil. Refrigerate for at least 2 hours, if possible with a weight on top, then cut into 10cm (4in) pieces. Wrap each piece separately and return to the refrigerator until required for school.
Makes about 12

Scotch Eggs

500g (1lb) sausagemeat

2 tblspn chopped fresh parsley

1 tspn mild curry powder or salt and pepper

1 egg, lightly beaten

60ml (2fl oz) milk

60g (2oz) flour

125g (4oz) dried white breadcrumbs

4 hard-boiled eggs

oil for deep frying

1 Combine the sausagemeat, parsley and curry powder or salt and pepper in a bowl. Divide into 4 portions and pat each portion out to a round about 12cm (5in) in diameter.

2 Beat egg and milk in a shallow bowl. Spread out flour in a second bowl and breadcrumbs in a third.

3 Dip hard-boiled eggs in milk mixture, then roll them in flour, shaking off excess. Place each egg in turn on a sausagemeat round, moulding sausagemeat evenly around egg and pinching it together to seal joins.

4 Dip the eggs into milk mixture again and roll in breadcrumbs.

5 Deep fry over moderate heat for about 10 minutes until the crumb coating on each egg is golden brown and the sausagemeat is cooked. When cold, wrap each egg separately and refrigerate until required. Use within 24 hours of making.
Makes 4

Health Tip
Foods such as bananas, oranges, tangerines and washed apples or carrots make ideal additions to packed lunches. Limit foods that are high in fat or sugar. Offer small boxes of dried fruits instead of sweets; slices of homemade fruit cake instead of chocolate snack bars. Salads are ideal lunchbox fare.

Scotch Eggs

Cheddar and Ham Cheesecake

125g (4oz) plain cheese biscuits

125g (4oz) butter, melted

3 eggs, lightly beaten

125g (4oz) cream cheese

125ml (4fl oz) soured cream

125g (4oz) Cheddar cheese, grated

1/2 tspn freshly grated nutmeg

60g (2oz) cooked ham, chopped

1 Preheat oven to 180°C (350°F/Gas 4). Process biscuits in a blender or food processor, or crush them by hand. Combine biscuit crumbs and melted butter in a medium bowl; mix well.

2 Using a spoon, press mixture firmly onto base and sides of a 20cm (8in) loose-based flan tin. Refrigerate while making filling.

3 Combine eggs, cream cheese, soured cream, Cheddar cheese and nutmeg in a blender or food processor. Process until quite smooth. Alternatively, mix ingredients in a bowl, then press them through a sieve into a large jug. Stir in ham.

4 Pour mixture into prepared flan tin. Bake for 30 minutes. Cool, then cut in slices and refrigerate until required for school.
Serves 6

Kitchen Tip
Packed lunches may have to stand for several hours before being eaten. Ideally, they should be freshly prepared each morning, but many items can be safely packed the night before and refrigerated until required. Store raw and cooked foods separately, and use insulated lunch boxes if possible. Avoid packing cooked meats or fish if the weather is hot.

Fruity Slice

250g (8oz) sugar

250g (8oz) butter or margarine

185g (6oz) sultanas

185g (6oz) dried apricots, finely chopped

2 eggs, beaten

125g (4oz) self-raising flour

125g (4oz) wholemeal self-raising flour

1 tspn mixed spice

1 Preheat oven to 180°C (350°F/Gas 4). Combine sugar and butter or margarine in a medium saucepan. Heat until butter melts. Off heat, add sultanas, apricots and eggs. Mix well.

2 Sift flours into a bowl; return husks from sieve to bowl. Add mixed spice, then gradually stir flour mixture into butter fruit mixture.

3 Spread the mixture in a greased Swiss roll tin and bake for 20 minutes. When cool, cut into squares. Store in an airtight container. Wrap in foil for school.
Makes 12 squares

Brownies

125g (4oz) butter

125g (4oz) dark chocolate, in squares

4 eggs

1/2 tspn salt

375g (12oz) sugar

2 tspn vanilla essence

125g (4oz) flour

125g (4oz) walnuts, roughly chopped

1 Preheat oven to 180°C (350°F/Gas 4). Combine the butter and chocolate in the top of a double boiler. Heat over simmering water until melted; set aside to cool.

2 In a bowl, beat the eggs with the salt, sugar and vanilla until lightly and fluffy. Quickly add the chocolate mixture, then fold in the flour and chopped walnuts.

3 Spread the mixture in a greased 33 x 23cm (13 x 9in) tin and bake for 25 minutes. Cut into squares when cool. Store in an airtight container. Wrap in foil for school.
Makes about 30 squares

Carob Oat Bars

110g (3 1/2oz) rolled oats

125g (4oz) flour

90g (3oz) soft brown sugar

60g (2oz) chopped hazelnuts

1 x 90g (3oz) carob bar, chopped

125g (4oz) butter, melted

3 tblspn clear honey

1 Preheat oven to 180°C (350°F /Gas 4). Combine all the ingredients in a bowl; mix well.

2 Press the mixture into a greased 20cm (8in) square baking tin. Bake for 25 minutes. Cool, then slice into bars and store in an airtight container.
Makes about 16 bars

Variations

Substitute 90g (3oz) chocolate chips for the carob, and use chopped walnuts instead of hazelnuts. Treacle or golden syrup may be used instead of the honey, and packaged muesli in place of the rolled oats.

Peanut Butter Biscuits

250g (8oz) butter, softened

250g (8oz) granulated sugar

250g (8oz) soft brown sugar

315g (10oz) crunchy peanut butter

2 eggs, beaten

315g (10oz) flour

3/4 tspn bicarbonate of soda

pinch salt

1 tspn vanilla essence

1 Combine the butter, sugars and peanut butter in a bowl. Beat until well mixed and soft. Beat in eggs.

2 Sift the flour, bicarbonate of soda and salt into the bowl. Add the vanilla and knead to a soft biscuit dough.

3 On a lightly floured surface divide the dough in half and roll each half to a cylinder. Wrap the cylinders in foil and refrigerate for at least 2 hours and up to 24 hours, until firm.

4 Preheat oven to 180°C (350°F/Gas 4). Cut the dough rolls into 5mm (1/4in) slices, arrange on greased baking sheets and bake for 13-15 minutes until golden. Cool on wire racks, then store in airtight containers.
Makes about 50

Butterbake Biscuits

125g (4oz) butter

60g (2oz) icing sugar

1 tspn vanilla essence

125g (4oz) flour, sifted

2 tblspn caster sugar

1 Preheat oven to 180°C (350°F /Gas 4). Beat the butter, icing sugar and vanilla together until pale and creamy. Fold in the flour in two lots.

2 Using floured hands, roll level teaspoons of the mixture into balls. Place balls 4cm (1 1/2in) apart on lightly greased baking sheets.

3 Bake for 10-12 minutes until light golden in colour. Transfer biscuits to a wire rack, sprinkle with caster sugar and cool. Store in an airtight container.
Makes 25-30

Muesli Slice

125g (4oz) butter or margarine

2 tblspn clear honey

90g (3oz) soft brown sugar

125g (4oz) packaged muesli

45g (1½oz) desiccated coconut

60g (2oz) wholemeal flour

60g (2oz) flaked almonds

90g (3oz) dried currants

90g (3oz) dried apricots, chopped

2 eggs, lightly beaten

1 Preheat oven to 160°C (325°F/ Gas 3). Melt the butter and honey in a large saucepan. Remove from the heat and stir in the sugar, muesli, coconut, flour, almonds, currants and apricots. Mix well.

2 Stir in the eggs. Press the mixture into a greased 20cm (8in) square baking tin. Bake for 25-30 minutes. Cut into squares when cool. Store in an airtight container. Wrap in foil for school.
Makes 16

Wholemeal Date Scones

125g (4oz) wholemeal self-raising flour

125g (4oz) self-raising flour

30g (1oz) natural bran

60g (2oz) margarine

125g (4oz) dates, finely chopped

250ml (8fl oz) milk

1 Preheat oven to 190°C (375°F/ Gas 5). Sift flours into a bowl; return husks from sieve to bowl. Stir in bran, rub in margarine and add dates.

2 Make a well in the centre of the dry ingredients and add enough milk to make a soft, sticky dough.

3 Turn the dough onto a lightly floured surface and knead lightly until smooth. Pat out to a thickness of 1cm (½in) and cut into rounds with a 5cm (2in) cutter.

4 Arrange the scones on greased baking sheets and bake for 15 minutes until risen and golden brown. Cool on wire racks, then store in an airtight container.
Makes about 15

Muesli Slice

Catering for teenagers means providing hearty, healthy food which can be stretched when extras arrive unexpectedly, and can happily be left to simmer when teenagers fail to pitch up on time. Chilli con Carne and Spinach and Cheese Lasagne fit the bill and the chapter also includes super salads and low-calorie desserts for this health-conscious age group.

Black-eyed Beans with Sausages

315g (10oz) black-eyed beans, soaked overnight in cold water to cover

2 cloves garlic, crushed

1 bay leaf

2 tspn cinnamon

¼ tspn grated nutmeg

6 pork sausages

45g (1½oz) butter

125g (4oz) peperoni, finely sliced

3 tblspn chopped fresh parsley

1 Drain the beans and put them in a large saucepan with the garlic, bay leaf, cinnamon and nutmeg. Add water to cover, bring to the boil and boil vigorously for 10 minutes. Lower the heat and simmer for about 35 minutes or until soft. Drain well; discarding bay leaf.

2 Prick the sausages and grill them until cooked through. Cool slightly, then slice into rounds.

3 Melt the butter in a large deep frying pan, add the peperoni and fry until crisp. Add the sausage rounds and cook for 2 minutes more.

4 Add the beans to the pan, toss well until heated through, sprinkle with parsley and serve at once.

Serves 6

Lamb and Tomato Curry

8 lamb chump chops

30g (1oz) butter

2 onions, roughly chopped

2 cloves garlic, crushed

2 tblspn mild curry powder

1 tspn cumin powder

2 x 397g (14oz) cans chopped tomatoes

2 apples, chopped

4 tblspn sultanas

4 tblspn slivered almonds

1 Cut away flesh from lamb chops, discarding bones and excess fat. Cut meat into 2cm (¾in) cubes.

2 Melt the butter in a large saucepan. Add the onions and garlic and fry over moderate heat until tender.

3 Stir in the curry powder and cumin and cook for I minute, then add lamb and cook until lightly browned.

4 Add tomatoes with can juices and cook for 3 minutes. Stir in apples, sultanas and almonds. Cover the mixture and simmer, stirring occasionally, for 30 minutes or until lamb is cooked. Garnish with coriander and serve with brown rice, if liked.

Serves 4

Lamb and Tomato Curry

Crispy Wholemeal Pizza

90g (3oz) wholemeal flour

90g (3oz) flour

1 tspn sugar

1 x 7g (¹/₄oz) sachet easy blend dried yeast

4 tblspn oil

125ml (4fl oz) hot water

2 onions, chopped

2 cloves garlic, crushed

1 x 397g (14oz) can chopped tomatoes

1 tblspn chopped fresh basil or 1 tspn dried basil

2 small red chillies, seeded and chopped, optional

1 green pepper, sliced

1 x 339g (12oz) can pineapple chunks in natural juice, drained

6 stuffed green olives, sliced

250g (8oz) mozzarella cheese, thinly sliced

1 Sift the flours into a bowl. Stir in the sugar and yeast and make a well in the centre. Mix 2 tblspn of the oil with the hot water and add to the well. Mix to a soft dough, then knead on a lightly floured surface for 10 minutes. Place dough in an oiled bowl, cover and set aside until doubled in bulk. Knead until smooth, then roll out to fit a 30cm (12in) round pizza plate.

2 Preheat oven to 190°C (375°F/Gas 5). Heat the remaining oil in a frying pan and sauté the onions and garlic until tender. Add the tomatoes, with the can juices, with the basil and chillies, if using. Simmer, uncovered, until reduced and thickened, then spread over pizza base. Top with green pepper, pineapple, olives and mozzarella. Bake for 20 minutes or until crust is crisp and golden.

Serves 6

Savoury Macaroni and Mince Gratin

2 tblspn olive oil

1 onion, chopped

2 cloves garlic, crushed

500g (1lb) lean minced beef

salt

freshly ground black pepper

1 x 397g (14oz) can chopped tomatoes with herbs

125g (4oz) mushrooms, quartered, or halved if small

2 tblspn chopped fresh parsley

375g (12oz) elbow macaroni

30g (1oz) grated Parmesan cheese

1 Heat the oil in a large frying pan and fry the onion and garlic over moderate heat until tender but not browned. Add mince; sauté until brown all over, breaking up well with a wooden spoon. Reduce heat to moderately low, season with salt and pepper and continue to cook, stirring constantly, for 5 minutes.

2 Stir in chopped tomatoes, mushrooms and parsley. With a slotted spoon, transfer half the mixture to an ovenproof serving dish.

3 Preheat oven to 200°C (400°F/Gas 60). Cook the macaroni in plenty of boiling salted water until tender or *al dente*. Drain, then place on top of the meat mixture. Top with the remaining meat mixture, sprinkle with Parmesan cheese and bake for 30 minutes. Serve.

Serves 4

Cheese and Pitta Strips

4 white pitta breads

125g (4oz) butter, melted

3 cloves garlic, crushed

2 tblspn chopped fresh basil or parsley

30g (1oz) grated Parmesan cheese

1 Preheat oven to 180°C (350°F/Gas 4). Split pitta breads in half, then cut each half into 3 strips.

2 Combine the butter, garlic and basil or parsley in a bowl. Brush over cut side of pitta strips; sprinkle with Parmesan cheese.

3 Arrange the pitta strips in a single layer on 2-3 baking sheets. Bake for 10 minutes or until crisp.

Makes 24 strips

Chilli con Carne

2 tblspn oil

2 onions, chopped

2 cloves garlic, crushed

1-2 tspn chilli powder

500g (1lb) lean minced beef

3 tblspn tomato purée

125ml (4fl oz) beef stock

1 x 397g (14oz) can chopped tomatoes

1 x 397g (14oz) can red kidney beans, rinsed and drained

125g (4oz) Cheddar cheese, grated

150ml (5fl oz) soured cream

1 Heat the oil in a large frying pan over moderate heat. Add the onions, garlic and chilli powder. Cook, stirring, for 2 minutes.

2 Add the minced beef and cook, stirring constantly, until well browned.

3 Stir in the tomato purée, stock, tomatoes with can juices and beans. Simmer for 30 minutes, stirring occasionally. Serve, topped with cheese and soured cream.

Serves 4

Chilli con Carne

Spinach and Cheese Lasagne

250g (8oz) spinach

500g (1lb) ricotta cheese

125g (4oz) mozzarella cheese, grated

2 spring onions, chopped

1 tspn dried basil

1 tspn dried oregano

2 tblspn chopped fresh parsley

1 tblspn oil

1 onion, chopped

1 carrot, chopped

1 stick celery, thinly sliced

1 clove garlic, crushed

2 x 397g (14oz) cans chopped tomatoes with herbs

3 tblspn tomato purée

1 bay leaf

125ml (4fl oz) chicken stock or white wine

3 tblspn grated Parmesan cheese

6 sheets no-precook lasagne

1 Boil, steam or microwave spinach until wilted. Drain well, then chop finely and put into a bowl.

2 Add the ricotta, mozzarella, spring onions, basil, oregano and parsley; mix well.

3 Heat the oil in a saucepan. Add the onion, carrot and celery and cook for 2 minutes, then add the garlic and cook for 1 minute more.

4 Stir in the tomatoes, tomato purée, bay leaf and stock or wine. Bring to the boil, lower the heat and simmer for 30 minutes. Remove bay leaf. If a smooth sauce is preferred, purée in a blender or food processor until smooth.

5 Preheat oven to 180°C (350°F/Gas 4). Spread one third of the tomato sauce on the base of a 33 x 28cm (13 x 11in) baking dish. Top with 3 sheets of lasagne, then spread half the spinach and ricotta mixture on top. Repeat the layers once more, then top with the remaining tomato sauce and sprinkle with Parmesan cheese. Cover the dish with foil.

6 Bake the lasagne in the oven for 40 minutes, removing the foil halfway through cooking. Allow to stand for 10 minutes before serving with a green salad. Offer extra grated Parmesan if liked.
Serves 4-6

Tortellini with Butter

Try to obtain Parmesan cheese in the piece for this recipe, and grate it freshly just before using.

2 tblspn olive oil

500g (1lb) tortellini

90g (3oz) Parmesan cheese, grated

125g (4oz) butter, cut into small cubes

1/4 tspn grated nutmeg

2 tblspn chopped fresh parsley

parsley sprig for garnish

1 Bring a large saucepan of water to the boil over moderate heat. Add the olive oil and tortellini and cook until the tortellini begin to float to the surface and are cooked through. Drain thoroughly.

2 Place the tortellini in a large heated serving bowl. Add the Parmesan cheese, butter, nutmeg and parsley. Toss gently until the butter has melted. Serve at once, garnished with the parsley sprig.
Serves 4

Tortellini with Butter

Crispy Baked Cod

Crispy Baked Cod

750g (1¹/₂lb) cod fillets, skinned and cut into 3.5cm (1¹/₂in) pieces

freshly ground black pepper

3 tblspn oil

30g (1oz) cornflakes, crumbed

1 tblspn lemon juice

lemon quarter slices, thin red pepper strips and dill for garnish

1 Preheat oven to 190°C (375°F/Gas 5). Rinse fish and pat dry with paper towels. Season with pepper and toss in oil. Lightly coat each fish piece with cornflake crumbs.

2 Arrange the fish pieces in a single layer on a lightly oiled baking dish. Bake for 10 minutes or until cooked.

3 Sprinkle the lemon juice over, garnish as in the illustration above, and serve.

Serves 6

Pork with Apricot Sauce

1 x 410g (13oz) can apricots

2 tspn cornflour

2 tspn soy sauce

1 tspn grated fresh root ginger

1 clove garlic, crushed

500g (1lb) pork fillet, trimmed

1 Preheat oven to 180°C (350°F/Gas 4). Drain the apricots, reserving 4 tblspn of the can juices. Purée the apricots with the juices in a blender or food processor. Add the cornflour, soy sauce, ginger and garlic and mix until smooth.

2 Place the pork fillet in a baking dish, pour over the apricot mixture and bake for 40 minutes. Remove the fillet, cut it into 1cm (¹/₂in) slices and arrange on a serving dish. Strain the sauce, pour it over the pork slices and serve at once.

Serves 4

Golden Chicken Sticks

1kg (2lb) chicken breast fillets

30g (1oz) flour

oil for deep frying

Dipping Sauce

3 tblspn tomato ketchup

2 tblspn red wine vinegar

2 tblspn soft brown sugar

2 tblspn fruit chutney

2 tspn cornflour dissolved in 1 tbspn soy sauce

350ml (12fl oz) water

1 Make sauce. Mix all ingredients in a saucepan. Bring to the boil, stirring constantly. Boil for 2 minutes, reduce heat and simmer while cooking the chicken.

2 Cut chicken into 7.5 x 1cm (3 x ¹/₂in) strips. Toss in flour, shaking off excess. Deep fry in batches until golden and crisp. Drain on paper towels. Serve chicken with sauce.

Makes about 20

Artichoke, Ham and Fresh Bean Salad

315g (10oz) fresh green beans

6 drained canned artichoke hearts, halved

155g (5oz) cooked ham, finely sliced into strips

2 tblspn finely chopped red pepper

10 walnut pieces

2 tspn walnut oil

1 tblspn freshly squeezed lime juice

coriander sprig for garnish

1 Top and tail the beans and cut them into 2cm (³/₄in) lengths. Cook beans in boiling water for 1 minute. Drain and refresh under cold running water. Drain thoroughly.

2 Arrange cold beans, artichoke hearts, ham, red pepper and walnuts on a serving dish.

3 Combine walnut oil and lime juice in a small bowl and whisk to combine. Pour over salad, garnish with coriander and serve.
Serves 4

Tossed Egg and Mushroom Salad

1 soft round lettuce

125g (4oz) cherry tomatoes

4 hard-boiled eggs, sliced

60g (2oz) mushrooms, sliced

1 tblspn snipped chives

1 avocado, sliced

1 clove garlic, crushed

1 tblspn red wine vinegar

2 tblspn orange juice

1 Tear lettuce into pieces and arrange in a salad bowl, with the tomatoes, egg slices, mushrooms, chives and avocado.

2 Mix together garlic, vinegar and orange juice, pour over salad, toss lightly and serve.
Serves 4

Tossed Egg and Mushroom Salad, Tossed Salad with Lemon Dressing

2 Make the dressing by mixing all the ingredients in a screwtop jar. Close the lid tightly. Shake the dressing vigorously until well mixed.

3 Pour enough of the dressing over the salad to coat well. Cover and set aside for 2 hours at cold room temperature.

4 Serve the salad on a bed of lettuce leaves.

Serves 4

Tossed Salad with Lemon Dressing

1 radicchio lettuce

1 soft round lettuce

1 red apple, thinly sliced

1 fennel bulb, trimmed, thinly sliced

60g (2oz) watercress sprigs

juice of 1 lemon

Tear lettuce leaves into pieces and arrange in a salad bowl with the apple slices, fennel and watercress. Pour lemon juice over salad and serve.

Serves 4

Tomato and Onion Salad

2 large tomatoes, sliced

1 red onion, sliced, separated into rings

60ml (2fl oz) natural low fat yogurt

60ml (2fl oz) tomato juice

1/2 tspn lemon juice

1/4 tspn soy sauce

salt

freshly ground black pepper

1 Arrange concentric circles of tomato slices and onion rings on a large salad plate.

2 Mix yogurt, tomato juice, lemon juice and soy sauce in a small bowl. Add salt and pepper to taste. Drizzle over salad, cover and set aside for 30 minutes before serving.

Serves 4

Provençal Salad

1 x 200g (6¹/₂oz) can tuna, drained and flaked

1 red pepper, cut into strips

1 green pepper, cut into strips

125g (4oz) French beans, cut into 2.5cm (1in) lengths, blanched

4 cherry tomatoes, halved

1 large cold boiled potato, diced

2 spring onions, diced

2 hard-boiled eggs, quartered

crisp lettuce leaves to serve

Dressing

4 cloves garlic, bruised

250ml (8fl oz) olive oil

1 tblspn finely chopped fresh parsley

1 tblspn snipped chives

1 tspn Dijon mustard

juice of 1 lemon

salt

freshly ground black pepper

1 Arrange the tuna, red and green pepper strips, beans, tomatoes, potato, spring onions and eggs in a bowl.

Chocolate Tart

Pastry

125g (4oz) flour

30g (1oz) cocoa, plus extra for dusting

90g (3oz) chilled butter, cut into small cubes

2 tblspn soft brown sugar

1 egg yolk

2 tspn white vinegar

2 tblspn iced water

Filling

250ml (8fl oz) canned custard

200g (6¹/₂oz) dark chocolate, melted

250ml (8fl oz) double cream

3 tblspn icing sugar

2 tblspn powdered gelatine

3 tblspn cold water

Topping

90g (3oz) dark chocolate

15g (¹/₂oz) butter

1 Combine flour and cocoa in a mixing bowl and rub in butter until mixture resembles fine breadcrumbs. Stir in sugar. Mix egg yolk, vinegar and iced water together and add to the flour to make a dough. Wrap in foil and chill for 30 minutes.

2 Preheat oven to 190°C (375°F/Gas 5). Dust work surface with cocoa and roll out pastry to fit a 23cm (9in) pie dish. Line pastry case with foil, then add baking beans. Bake for 10 minutes, remove foil and beans, and return pastry case to the oven for l0 minutes more. Cool completely.

3 Make the filling. Put the custard in a bowl and beat with a hand-held electric mixer. Still beating, add melted chocolate, then cream and icing sugar. Sprinkle the gelatine onto the water in a small bowl. When spongy, melt over hot water (or microwave on High for about 20 seconds). Stir into chocolate custard mixture.

4 Pour the mixture into the cooled pastry shell; chill until set. Make the topping by melting the chocolate with the butter in the top of a double boiler over simmering water. Quickly spread over the top of the pie, using a spatula. Chill before serving.
Serves 8

Kitchen Tip

The pastry can be made in a food processor. Use the metal blade and process all the ingredients together for about 10 seconds or until mixture forms a ball.

Fruit Kebabs with Honey Cream

250g (8oz) strawberries

1 small cantaloupe

4 kiwi fruit

250ml (8fl oz) soured cream

250ml (8fl oz) double cream

2 tblspn clear honey

2 tblspn chopped fresh mint

1 Prepare the fruit according to type; cut it into bite-sized pieces. Thread onto bamboo skewers or cocktail sticks.

2 Combine the soured cream, double cream, honey and mint in a bowl. Mix well. Set the bowl in the centre of a serving plate and arrange the fruit skewers around the sides for dipping.
Makes 16

Fruit Kebabs with Honey Cream

PARTY TIME

Tots and teenagers alike prefer no-fuss finger food as party fare. Spareribs, sausage puffs, chicken bites feature alongside sandwich spirals, dips and both sweet and savoury fondues in a chapter that's full of entertaining ideas.

Honey Glazed Spareribs

16 meaty pork spareribs, trimmed of excess fat

350ml (12fl oz) rice wine vinegar or cider vinegar

125ml (4fl oz) soy sauce

125ml (4fl oz) clear honey

2 spring onions, finely chopped

3 cloves garlic, chopped

1 tblspn grated fresh root ginger

Sauce

2 tblspn oil

2 onions, finely chopped

250ml (8fl oz) chicken stock

2 tblspn lemon juice

2 tblspn chopped fresh parsley

125g (4oz) butter

1 Place ribs in a single layer in a large shallow dish.

2 Combine vinegar, soy sauce, honey, spring onions, garlic and ginger in a jug; mix well. Pour mixture over spareribs, cover and refrigerate for at least 4 hours, preferably overnight.

3 Preheat oven to 150°C (300°F/Gas 2). Spread out ribs in a roasting tin, reserving marinade. Cook for 1 hour, basting occasionally with a little of the reserved marinade.

4 When ribs are almost cooked, make sauce. Heat oil in a saucepan and fry onions for 3-4

Honey Glazed Spareribs

minutes. Add remaining marinade with stock, lemon juice and parsley. Bring to the boil, lower the heat and simmer for 15 minutes or until reduced by half.

5 Remove ribs from oven and finish cooking them over a barbecue or under a hot grill.

6 Melt butter in a small saucepan. Pour sauce mixture into a blender or food processor and purée until smooth. With the motor running, pour in the hot melted butter in a steady stream.

7 Cut ribs into short lengths and serve with sauce.
Serves 8

Cheesy Potato Chips

500g (1lb) potatoes

60ml (2fl oz) oil

4 tblspn grated Parmesan cheese

4 tblspn sesame seeds

salt to serve

1 Preheat oven to 240°C (475°F/Gas 8). Peel potatoes and cut into 1cm (1/2in) thick chips. Dry well with kitchen towels. Spread chips in a roasting tin, sprinkle with oil and turn to coat. Sprinkle with the cheese and sesame seeds.

2 Bake for 40 minutes or until chips are golden brown and cooked through, turning the chips halfway through cooking. Drain on paper towels and serve with a little salt.
Serves 4

Curried Sausage Puffs

1 x 368g (13oz) packet frozen puff pastry, thawed

500g (1lb) sausagemeat

1 small carrot, finely grated

2 spring onions, finely chopped

2 tblspn fruit chutney

2 tspn curry powder

2 tblspn natural bran

freshly ground black pepper

1 Preheat oven to 200°C (400°F/Gas 6). On a lightly floured surface, roll out the pastry thinly to a rectangle measuring about 35 x 25cm (14 x 10in).

2 Mix all remaining ingredients in a bowl, then divide mixture into 4 equal parts. With floured hands, shape one portion into a thin sausage about 35cm (14in) in length. Place this along long side of the pastry, folding enough pastry over to enclose it and make a long sausage roll. Seal join. Cut away excess pastry. Repeat with remaining mixture to make 4 rolls. Cut each roll into 1cm (¹/₂in) slices, arrange on baking sheets and bake for 15 minutes or until golden.
Makes about 60

Nutty Chicken Breasts

125g (4oz) walnuts, finely chopped

60g (2oz) fresh breadcrumbs

4 large chicken breast fillets

2 tblspn Dijon mustard

2 eggs, lightly beaten

125ml (4fl oz) oil

100g (3¹/₂oz) butter

1 Combine nuts and bread-crumbs. Spread each chicken breast with mustard, dip in the egg and coat with nut mixture. Place on a plate and chill for 1 hour.

2 Heat oil and butter in a large frying pan over moderate heat. Fry chicken breasts until golden brown and cooked through. Drain on paper towels.
Serves 4

Swiss Cheese Fondue

1 clove garlic, crushed

500g (1lb) Gruyère cheese, grated

3 tblspn potato flour

185ml (6fl oz) dry white wine, alcohol free if preferred

blanched broccoli and cauliflower florets, whole button mushrooms, baby corn cobs and cubes of day-old bread for dipping

1 Rub around the inside of a fondue pot with the crushed garlic. Add the cheese, flour and wine.

2 Cook over moderate heat until cheese has melted and mixture is thick and creamy.

3 Serve at once, with vegetables on skewers or toothpicks for dipping.
Serves 4-8

Tacos with Salmon and Avocado

10 taco shells

1 x 440g (14oz) can red salmon, drained

1 red pepper, finely chopped

1 onion, thinly sliced

60ml (2fl oz) French dressing

1 large avocado, chopped

1 tblspn lemon juice

1 small lettuce, shredded

60g (2oz) beansprouts

1 Heat taco shells according to packet instructions.

2 Remove skin and bones from salmon, break into chunks and combine with pepper, onion and dressing in a bowl.

3 Toss avocado in lemon juice; add to salmon mixture.

4 Fill taco shells with lettuce, salmon mixture and bean-sprouts. Serve immediately.
Makes 10

Guacamole

Guacamole

3 avocados, halved, seeded and peeled

2 small tomatoes, peeled

1 small onion, very finely chopped

2-3 red chillies, seeded and chopped

2 tblspn chopped fresh coriander

2 tblspn lemon juice

2 x 200g (6¹/₂oz) packets corn chips

1 Put avocado flesh in a bowl and mash. Cut tomatoes into quarters, remove and discard seeds. Cut tomato flesh into small dice.

2 Combine avocado, tomato, onion, chillies, coriander and lemon juice. Mix well, spoon into a serving bowl and serve with corn chips for dipping.

Serves 8

Kitchen Tip

When chopping the chillies, take great care to avoid touching your lips or eyes, or a reaction may occur. Wash your hands carefully after handling the chillies.

Egg and Spring Onion Spirals

1 (unsliced) loaf wholemeal bread

125g (4oz) butter, softened

8 hard-boiled eggs

2 tblspn mayonnaise

2 tblspn soured cream

4 spring onions, finely chopped

2 tspn dry mustard

1 Remove crusts from loaf of bread; cut lengthwise into 6 slices. Butter each slice.

2 In a bowl, mash eggs finely. Stir in mayonnaise, soured cream, spring onions and mustard. Spread evenly over each bread slice.

3 Roll up each bread slice from a long edge. Wrap firmly in cling film, refrigerate for 1-2 hours. Serve sliced.

Makes about 48 spirals

Banana Clock Cake

250g (8oz) butter, softened

185g (6oz) soft brown sugar

4 eggs

4 bananas, mashed

250ml (8fl oz) soured cream

125ml (4fl oz) oil

500g (1lb) self-raising flour, sifted

1 tblspn mixed spice

Icing

250g (8oz) butter, softened

500g (1lb) icing sugar

1 tblspn milk

food colouring

Decoration

90g (3oz) desiccated coconut, coloured if liked

hundreds and thousands

licorice bootlaces and strips

candy-coated chocolate buttons

assorted small sweets

1 Preheat oven to 180°C (350°F/Gas 4). In a mixing bowl, cream butter and sugar. Add eggs, one at a time, beating well after each addition. Stir in the bananas, soured cream and oil.

2 Fold in the flour and spice. Divide the mixture between two greased 20cm (8in) cake tins. Bake for 30-35 minutes or until an inserted skewer comes out clean. Cool on wire racks.

3 Make the icing. Beat butter, icing sugar and milk in a bowl until creamy. Divide mixture in half, tinting one half pale yellow and the other pink; add colouring drop by drop until the desired intensity is achieved. (Icing darkens slightly after 1 hour on cake.) Cover until ready to use.

4 Cut one cake layer as shown in sketch opposite. Assemble.

5 Cover top and sides of other cake with yellow icing; sprinkle cake with coconut. Ice 'peak of clock' with pink icing; carefully position above the clock face.

6 Cover each mouse with pink icing and roll in hundreds and thousands. Make tails and whiskers from licorice bootlaces. Cut numerals and mouse ears from licorice strips. Decorate rest of clock as desired.
Serves 12

Funny Faces

Children love to make these treats. They can be prepared up to 2 hours before serving.

250g (8oz) low fat cream cheese

1 tspn grated lemon rind

24 digestive biscuits

licorice, candy-coated chocolate buttons, jelly beans, hundreds and thousands, vermicelli and other small sweets for decoration

1 Beat the cream cheese with the lemon rind and sugar until smooth. Top each biscuit with a little of the mixture.

2 Use sweets (and imagination) to make faces. Allow to set for 30 minutes before serving.
Makes 24

Banana Clock Cake, Funny Faces

Buttery Fudge

150ml (5fl oz) sweetened condensed milk

150ml (5fl oz) milk

125g (4oz) butter

440g (14oz) caster sugar

few drops vanilla essence

1 Combine the ingredients in a heavy-based saucepan. Stir over low heat until sugar has completely dissolved, then raise heat and boil, stirring constantly, until mixture registers 120°C (250°F/Gas ½) on a sugar thermometer. Remove from the heat and stir briskly for at least 3 minutes.

2 Pour mixture into a buttered 30 x 20cm (12 x 8in) cake tin. When nearly cool and set, cut into squares with a sharp knife.
Makes 32 squares

Kitchen Tip

If you do not have a sugar thermometer, boil the mixture until it starts to come away from the sides of the pan. Test by dropping a little of the mixture into a cup of cold water; if it forms a soft ball, the fudge is ready to be removed from the heat. Brisk stirring at this stage makes it creamy.

Peanut and Honey Popcorn

1 tblspn oil

60g (2oz) popcorn kernels

2 tblspn peanut butter

2 tblspn honey

2 tblspn sesame seeds

1 Heat oil in a saucepan, add popcorn, cover and cook over moderate heat until all the kernels have popped. Remove popcorn, draining off any oil.

2 Mix peanut butter, honey and sesame seeds in a saucepan. Heat gently until smooth, add popcorn and stir until coated. Serve.
Serves 6

Chocolate Nut Clusters

315g (10oz) dark chocolate, in squares

220g (7oz) nibbed almonds

45g (1½oz) desiccated coconut

1 Melt chocolate in a bowl over a saucepan of simmering water; stir in almonds and coconut.

2 Place heaped spoonfuls onto a lightly greased baking sheet and allow to set.
Makes about 24

Fruit Salad Jelly Mould with Apricot Sauce

Jelly gets a new lease of life in this colourful dessert. Vary the fruit to make the best of seasonal varieties.

2 tspn powdered gelatine

1 x 90g (3oz) packet jelly crystals (any flavour)

250ml (8fl oz) water

750ml (1¼pt) apple juice

3 tblspn freshly squeezed orange juice

2 tblspn lemon juice

375g (12oz) strawberries, hulled and halved

4 kiwi fruit, peeled and sliced

Sauce

375g (12oz) apricots, stoned and chopped

125g (4oz) apricot jam

5 tblspn water

1 Sprinkle the gelatine and jelly crystals onto the water in a medium bowl. Melt over hot water, stirring until dissolved. Cool slightly, then stir in the apple juice, orange juice and lemon juice. Set aside.

2 Lightly oil a 1.5 litre (2½pt) mould. Arrange half the strawberries and kiwi fruit on the base, gently pour over half the jelly mixture and chill until set.

3 Arrange the remaining fruit on top of the chilled jelly; pour over the remaining jelly mixture. Refrigerate for several hours or until set.

4 To make the sauce, combine the apricots, jam and water in a small saucepan. Simmer for 5 minutes, then press the mixture through a sieve into a jug. Serve with the unmoulded jelly.

Serves 6-8

White Chocolate Fondue

250g (8oz) white chocolate, chopped

185ml (6fl oz) double cream

250g (8oz) strawberries, hulled and quartered

60g (2oz) marshmallows, halved

125g (4oz) green seedless grapes

grated dark chocolate to decorate

1 Combine the chocolate and cream in a medium saucepan. Heat gently, stirring constantly until chocolate has melted and mixture is smooth. Pour into a serving bowl and set aside to cool to room temperature.

2 Thread strawberries, marsh-mallows and grapes onto wooden skewers or toothpicks. Serve with the chocolate fondue.

Serves 8

White Chocolate Fondue

Chocolate Eclairs

Choux Pastry

50g (2oz) butter, chopped
250ml (8fl oz) water
125ml (4fl oz) flour
2 eggs, plus 1 egg yolk

Filling and Topping

350ml (12fl oz) double cream
2 tblspn icing sugar
155g (5oz) milk chocolate
15g (1/2oz) butter

1 Preheat oven to 220°C (425°F/Gas 7). Make the choux pastry. Combine the butter and water in a medium saucepan over moderate heat. Bring to the boil, add the flour all at once and stir vigorously over moderate heat until the mixture leaves the sides of the pan and forms a smooth ball. Transfer to a mixing bowl and cool for 10 minutes. Beat in the egg yolk, then add the whole eggs, one at a time, beating well after each addition.

2 Using a large piping bag fitted with a plain nozzle, pipe 10cm (4in) lengths of the pastry onto greased baking sheets. Bake for 10 minutes, then lower the oven temperature to 180°C (350°F/Gas 4) and bake for 20 minutes more. Remove from the oven, split eclairs open and cool on a wire rack.

3 Make filling by beating cream and icing sugar together in a bowl until soft peaks form. Fill eclairs. Melt chocolate and butter in a bowl over hot water, stir, then drizzle over the tops of the eclairs.

Makes 10-12

Melon and Strawberry Salad

1 cantaloupe, cut into bite-sized chunks
1/2 honeydew melon, cut into bite-sized chunks
250g (8oz) strawberries, hulled and halved
2 tblspn grenadine syrup

Chocolate Eclairs

1 Combine the melon chunks and strawberries in a bowl. Pour over the grenadine and stir gently to mix.

2 Transfer to a serving bowl and chill before serving.

Serves 6

Almond Meringue Cookies

4 egg whites
185g (6oz) caster sugar
90g (3oz) ground almonds
1/2 tspn cream of tartar
25 blanched almond halves
250ml (8fl oz) double cream, whipped

1 Preheat oven to 160°C (325°F/Gas 3). Whisk the egg whites with the sugar until the mixture forms soft peaks. Fold in the ground almonds and cream of tartar.

2 Line 2 baking sheets with nonstick baking parchment. Drop teaspoonfuls of the mixture, 4cm (1 1/2in) apart on the baking sheets, and press an almond half onto the top of each biscuit. Bake for 20 minutes, then cool on baking sheets for 3 minutes before transferring biscuits to wire racks to cool completely.

3 Repeat the process until all the mixture has been used up, topping half the biscuits with an almond half, and leaving the remainder plain.

4 Sandwich the biscuits together with the whipped cream, using a plain biscuit for each base.

Makes about 25

Pineapple Soda

500ml (16fl oz) water

500g (1lb) sugar

500ml (16fl oz) unsweetened pineapple juice

250ml (8fl oz) lemon juice

500ml (16fl oz) chilled soda water

thin orange slices and mint sprigs to serve

1 Combine water and sugar in a saucepan. Heat, stirring, until sugar has dissolved, then bring to the boil. Lower the heat and simmer for 10 minutes; cool.

2 Stir in pineapple juice and lemon juice. Pour into a tall jug and add soda water. Stir lightly.

3 Serve in tall glasses filled with ice cubes and decorated with orange slices and mint sprigs.
Makes about 2 litres (3 1/2pt)

Kitchen Tip
Frosted glasses are fun. Dip rims of glasses in egg white, then in caster sugar. Allow to dry before carefully filling glasses.

Blackberry Cup

750g (1 1/2lb) frozen blackberries

125g (4oz) sugar

500ml (16fl oz) freshly squeezed orange juice

250ml (8fl oz) lemon juice

crushed ice

chilled soda water

1 Purée blackberries with sugar in a blender or food processor. Sieve into a saucepan. Bring to the boil over moderate heat.

2 Off the heat, add orange juice and lemon juice. Cool, then chill.

3 Half-fill tall glasses with crushed ice, fill three-quarters full with the blackberry mixture, then top up with soda water. Stir gently and serve.
Makes 8 drinks

Orange Honey Whip, Mango Milkshake

Orange Honey Whip

500ml (16fl oz) orange juice

4 seedless oranges, peeled and chopped

2 tblspn natural low fat yogurt

2 tblspn clear honey

Blend all the ingredients together in a blender or food processor until smooth. Strain into a jug; serve chilled.
Makes about 600ml (1pt)

Mango Milkshake

1 mango, peeled, flesh chopped

250ml (8fl oz) crushed ice

250ml (8fl oz) milk

Combine mango flesh, ice and milk in a blender or food processor; blend until smooth. Serve in tall glasses, decorated with a strip of kiwi fruit.
Makes about 600ml (1pt)

USEFUL INFORMATION

Length

Centimetres	Inches	Centimetres	Inches
0.5 (5mm)	1/4	18	7
1	1/2	20	8
2	3/4	23	9
2.5	1	25	10
4	1 1/2	30	12
5	2	35	14
6	2 1/2	40	16
7.5	3	45	18
10	4	50	20
15	6	NB: 1cm = 10 mm	

Metric/Imperial Conversion Chart

Mass (Weight)
(Approximate conversions for cookery purposes)

Metric	Imperial	Metric	Imperial
15g	1/2oz	315g	10oz
30g	1oz	350g	11oz
60g	2oz	375g	12oz (3/4lb)
90g	3oz	410g	13oz
125g	4oz (1/4lb)	440g	14oz
155g	5oz	470g	15oz
185g	6oz	500g (0.5kg)	16oz (1lb)
220g	7oz	750g	24oz (1 1/2lb)
250g	8oz (1/2lb)	1000g (1kg)	32oz (2lb)
280g	9oz	1500 (1.5kg)	3lb

Metric Spoon Sizes

1/4 teaspoon	= 1.25ml
1/2 teaspoon	= 2.5ml
1 teaspoon	= 5ml
1 tablespoon	=15ml

Liquids

Metric	Imperial
30ml	1fl oz
60 ml	2fl oz
90ml	3fl oz
125ml	4fl oz
155ml	5fl oz (1/4pt)
185ml	6fl oz
250ml	8fl oz
500ml	16fl oz
600ml	20fl oz (1pt)
750ml	1 1/4pt
1 litre	1 3/4pt
1.2 litres	2pt
1.5 litres	2 1/2pt
1.8 litres	3pt
2 litres	3 1/2pt
2.5 litres	4pt

Index

Editorial Coordination: Merehurst Limited
Cookery Editors: Jenni Fleetwood, Katie Swallow
Editorial Assistant: Sheridan Packer
Production Manager: Sheridan Carter
Layout and Finished Art: Stephen Joesph
Cover Photography: David Gill
Cover Design: Maggie Aldred

Published by J.B. Fairfax Press Pty Limited
80-82 McLachlan Avenue
Rushcutters Bay, NSW 2011
A.C.N. 003 738 430

Formatted by J.B. Fairfax Press Pty Limited
Printed by Toppan Printing Co, Singapore

JBFP 293 A/UK
Includes Index
ISBN 1 86343 116 0 (set)
ISBN 1 86343 132 2

Distribution and Sales Enquiries
Australia: J.B. Fairfax Press Pty Limited
Ph: (02) 361 6366 Fax: (02) 360 6262
United Kingdom: J.B. Fairfax Press Limited
Ph (0933) 402330 Fax (02) 402234